OUR WORLD

THEN & NOW

FIVE PONDS PRESS

OUR WORLD
THEN & NOW

by Joy Masoff

Unit 1: History

ADVISORY BOARD

Dr. Melissa Matusevich: Professor of Curriculum and Instruction at East Carolina University and former supervisor of Social Studies and Library Media, Montgomery County, Virginia, Public Schools.

Dr. Donald Zeigler: Professor of Geography and Political Science, Old Dominion University, Norfolk, Virginia.

REVIEWERS

Five Ponds Press wishes to acknowledge the contributions and encouragement of many Virginia public school educators. Special thanks to:
Kathy Morrison, Lead Teacher Specialist for Social Studies K-12, Hanover County Public Schools
Kathleen Nealon of Fairfax County
Nancy Maxwell of Fairfax County
Carol Padgett of Fairfax County
Anita Parker of Virginia Beach
Lara Samuels of Hanover County
Bree Linton, formerly of Hanover County
Michele Landry of Prince William County
and **Jason Deryck-Mahlke** of John Jay High School, NY

Copyright ©2005 by Joy Masoff. All rights reserved.
Published by Five Ponds Press, Waccabuc, NY 10597.
Library of Congress Cataloging-in-Publication data available.
First printing July 2005.

ISBN 0-9727156-6-5
Manufactured in the USA.

Unit 2: Geography

Unit 3: Economics

Unit 4: Civics

CHAPTER 1

Long Ago

In the past, life was very different.

Children did not have TV's or computers.

They did not shop at malls.

There were no cars to take

people places.

Past

Today

Life has changed!
We wear comfortable clothes.
We have lots of toys.

Present times are different from past times!

Present

Old Schools

Long ago, many schools had only one room.

First graders and high school kids sat side by side.

There was one teacher for everyone.

There were only a few books.

One Room

W.T. COOKE ELEMENTARY

NOW

New Schools

Today schools are much bigger.

Every grade has its own classrooms.

There are art and music teachers.

There are gyms and computer rooms.

There are libraries filled with books.

Many Rooms

THEN

Small Towns

Richmond, Virginia in 1850

Fewer People

Communities *(come-YOU-ni-tees)* are places
where people live, work, and play.
In the past, communities were smaller.
Buildings and shops were small too.
Firefighters put out fires with small trucks.

Big Cities

Richmond, Virginia today

More People

NOW

Communities have changed. Now many people live in big buildings. We shop in big malls. Firefighters need bigger trucks when there is a fire.

Going Slowly

THEN

Horses and Feet

Transportation (*trans-por-TAY-shun*) is the way we travel from place to place. Long ago, people walked or rode horses.

Horses pulled covered wagons. It took a long time to get places.

Going Fast

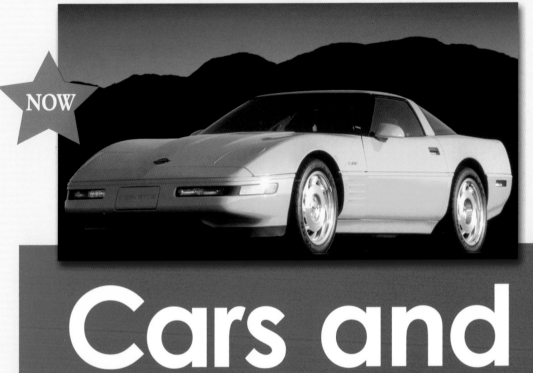

NOW

Cars and Planes

Today we have fast, shiny cars. There are buses and trains too. Planes cross the country in just a few hours. Space ships have flown to the moon! Transportation has changed a lot.

11

Made by Hand

Families (*FAM-ull-eez*) are groups of people who care for one another—moms and dads, sisters and brothers, grandmas and grandpas, aunts and uncles.

Long ago, families wore handmade clothes. They played homemade games.

Families grew their own food in backyard gardens or farms.

THEN

Family Then

Bought in Stores

Today most families buy clothes in stores.

Boys and girls play electronic games.

Kids love toys that need batteries, and they like to watch TV.

Moms, dads, and grandparents are so busy they often microwave dinner or go out to eat.

NOW

Family Now

Timeline

Columbus sails
to the New World.

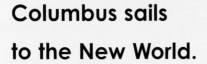

George
Washington leads
America during
the War for
Independence.

Abraham Lincoln
is President as
America fights
the Civil War.

1492

1776

1861

Timelines (*TIME-lines*) are a fun way to see how things have changed over many years. Look at this timeline. Which came first—George Washington or men walking on the moon?

Many Americans begin to buy cars.

A man walks on the moon.

Many families use computers.

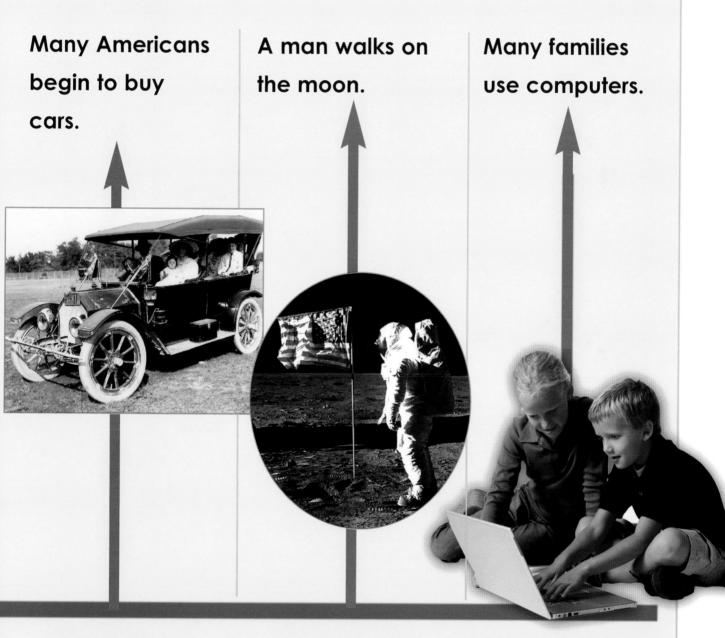

1927   1969   2000

CHAPTER 2

Great Americans

George Washington

When America asked him to help, George Washington said, "Yes." He never gave up, even if what he was doing was very hard. He was our country's first leader so we call him the "Father of Our Country."

George Washington was born in Virginia and grew up to be a farmer and a soldier. This is his house at Mount Vernon.

Washington led the army when America went to war against England. He was so brave!

After the war George Washington became the first President of our country—the brand-new United States. He helped our new country grow strong.

A True Leader

17

Benjamin Franklin

What is a **contribution** (*con-tri-BYU-shun*)? When you give or do something for another person, you have made a contribution. Benjamin Franklin made a lot of contributions. He invented things that made life easier. He helped others and also helped our nation.

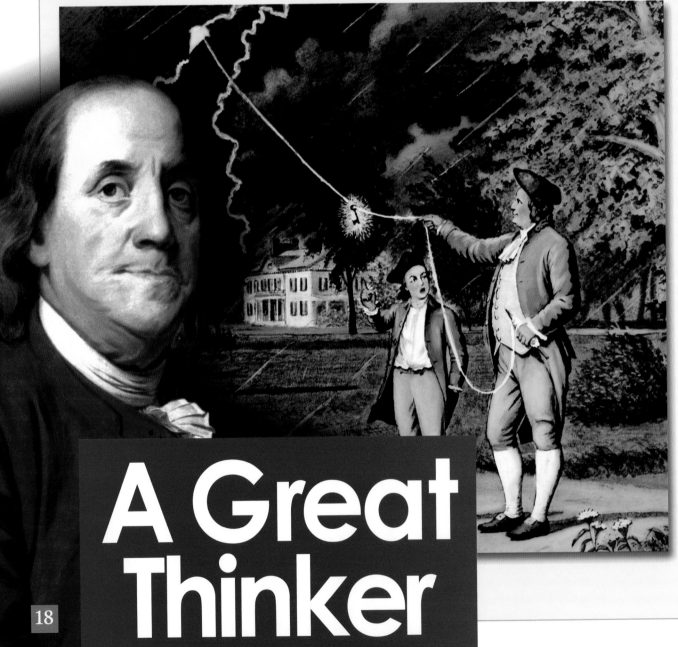

A Great Thinker

Benjamin Franklin was curious about the world. He flew a kite on a stormy night to prove that electricity was present in lightning.

Houses often burned down in Benjamin Franklin's time, so he started the very first volunteer fire department.

Benjamin Franklin also loved to read. He opened the first free library in America so people who could not afford to buy books could read too.

Benjamin Franklin helped America in many ways when it was a brand-new country.

Two of the many ways America has honored Franklin.

Honest Abe

As a boy, Lincoln lived in a log cabin like this one.

Abraham Lincoln

One of America's best-loved leaders was born in a tiny log cabin. Abraham Lincoln came from a poor family, but that did not stop him from becoming the 16th President of the United States.

Abraham Lincoln was very smart. He taught himself to read and worked hard at all sorts of jobs.

Lincoln worked as a fence builder and a river boat pilot. Lincoln also worked at a store. He got his nickname, "Honest Abe," working there. One day he made a mistake and charged someone too much money.

Lincoln walked many miles to give the man his change back. Soon people began talking about how honest Lincoln was.

In time, Lincoln became a lawyer. He did very well at this!

When Lincoln became President, the states began to fight. They could not agree on how the country should be run. The Civil War began, and America split in two.

Lincoln worked hard to bring the states back together.

George Washington Carver

Do you like peanut butter? George Washington Carver spent his life working with peanuts and many other plants. He also became a teacher.

A Man of Science

Carver was an African American who loved plants. He wanted to learn everything he could about plants, so he studied science. He was always asking questions.

Carver had so many great ideas. He came up with over 300 ways to use peanuts! He also made 108 products from sweet potatoes. He even learned how to make paint from soybeans.

George Washington Carver was a wonderful teacher and a great inventor.

NORMAL
PEANUT BUTTER
10 OZ NET WT

Holidays

Why do we have holidays?
A holiday is a day when we honor a person
or remember a special event.
Sometimes we
get the day off
from school for
a holiday!

What is your
favorite
holiday?
How many
holidays do
you know?

GOD BLESS AMERICA

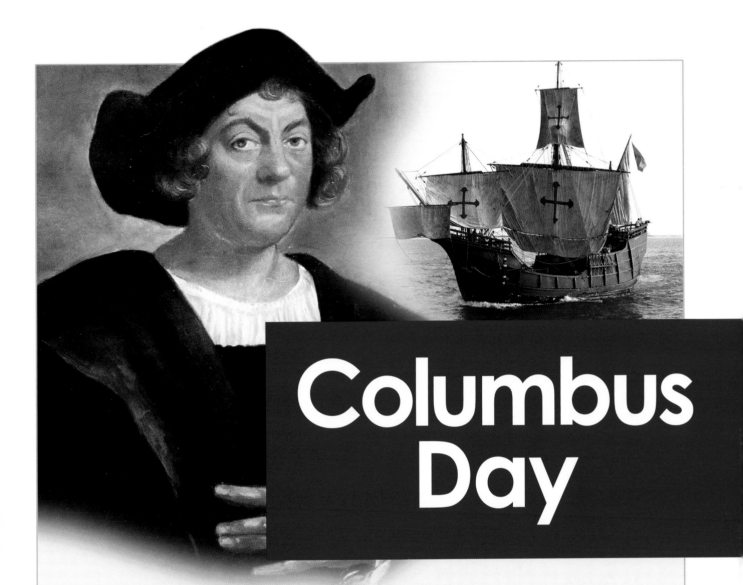

Columbus Day

In **October**, we remember **Christopher Columbus**.
In 1492, Columbus sailed across the Atlantic Ocean.
That October, he landed in a new world, America.
He then sailed back home and told everyone what
he had found.

Even though Columbus was not the first person to
come to America, he became famous for his trip.

An October Holiday

Presidents' Day

Two very great Presidents—George Washington and Abraham Lincoln—were both born in February. We honor them and all of America's Presidents on Presidents' Day.

A February Holiday

America's Birthday

July 4 is also called Independence Day.

Flags fly. Fireworks light up the sky.

We march in parades and have picnics.

It is America's birthday.

Long ago, on July 4, 1776, the United States became a new country.

The Fourth of July

4 Maps and Globes

If you were a bird, you might see the world like this.
Why do you think everything looks so small?

A map is a drawing that shows where a place is and
what it looks like from high above—the kind of view
a bird would see. Maps tell you where
things are.

This bald eagle is flying over a big city.

Where Are You?

A map of the world

There are two ways to look at the world from above—maps and globes. Maps are flat. They can show the whole world or a small part of it. Globes are round models of the Earth that show the way it looks from space. Globes always show the whole planet.

A globe of the world

The World

This map shows the whole world.

The Earth is covered with land and water.

There are seven very big pieces of land called continents *(CON-tin-ents)*.

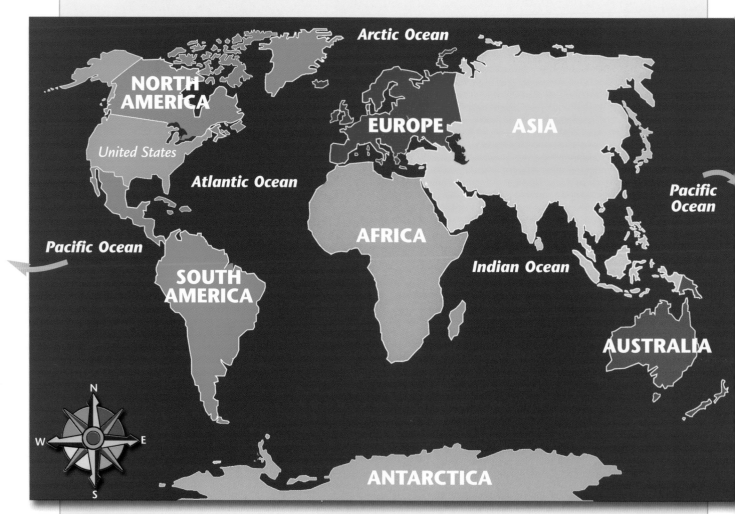

Seven Continents

Land and Water

We live on the continent of North America.
Can you find it on the map?

There are four big oceans (OH-shins).
Most maps show oceans with the
color blue—just like a lake or the sea.

These children are holding globes.
You have to turn a globe to
see all the continents.

*This girl has turned
her globe to show
Africa, Europe, and
Asia. The boy's
globe shows North
America.*

Alaska

Pacific Ocean

The United States

Atlantic Ocean

Hawaii

The **United States** is part of the continent of North America. Can you find it on the map? Can you find it on the globe?

The United States

There are 50 states in the United States. Two states, Alaska and Hawaii, are far away and do not touch the other 48 states. The 48 states that touch are called the continental United States. Virginia is our home state.

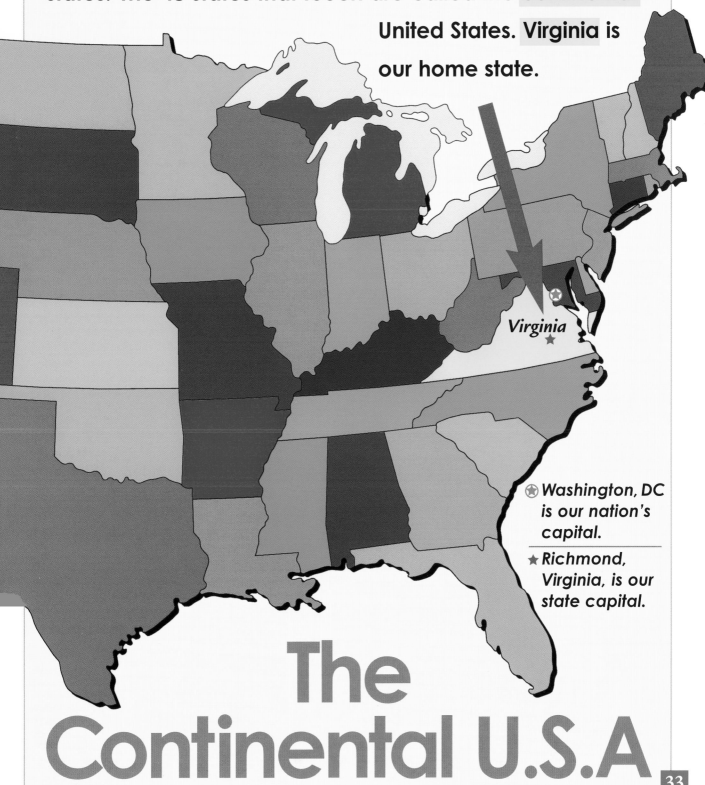

Virginia

⊛ Washington, DC is our nation's capital.

★ Richmond, Virginia, is our state capital.

The Continental U.S.A

Our State Map

We live in the state of Virginia. It is a great state. It has beaches, rivers, and mountains.

A lot of important things have happened in Virginia.

MAP LEGEND

 RIVER

STATE CAPITAL

 CITIES

UNITED STATES CAPITAL

AIRPORTS

 MOUNTAINS

This is a compass rose. It shows north, south, east, and west. These are called cardinal directions and help us find things on a map.

Virginia

MAP OF VIRGINIA

Washington,
D.C.

Chesapeake
Bay

James River

RICHMOND

Atlantic
Ocean

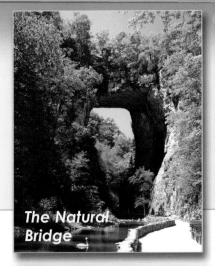

The Natural
Bridge

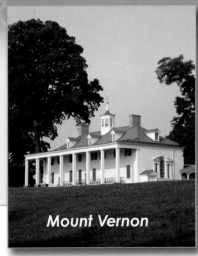

Mount Vernon

Our state capitol
building, in Richmond

35

Maps help us find our way around.
How do you make a map? You start by pretending that you are a bird who can draw!

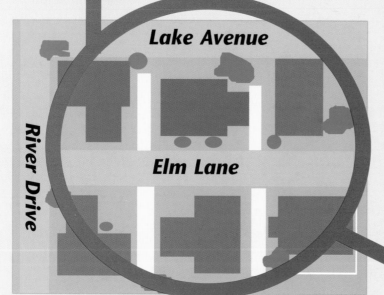

Lake Avenue

River Drive

Elm Lane

Look at this drawing. It is a map of the street at the top of this page.
It shows the houses, roads, and trees.

It is also part of a bigger map. Can you find it on the big map on the next page?

Map Parts

Drawing a Map

Maps use colors and symbols *(SIM-bulz)* to stand for something else. A symbol is a little picture or mark. A map legend lists the symbols.

Look at the map legend. Can you find the lake on the map? Can you find the school? What is west of the soccer field?

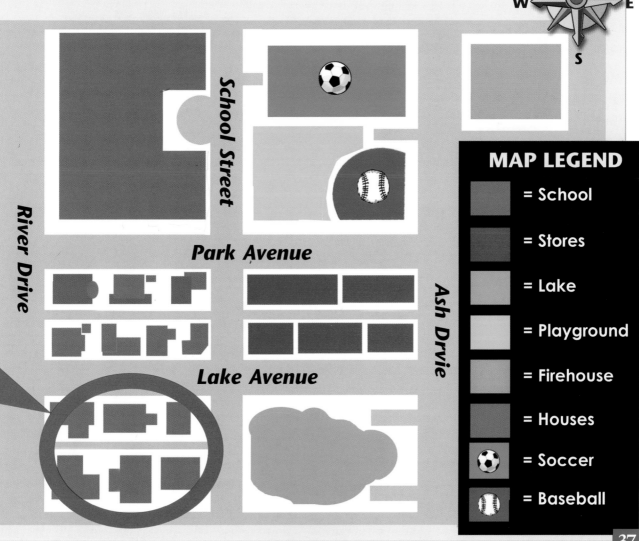

MAP LEGEND

= School

= Stores

= Lake

= Playground

= Firehouse

= Houses

= Soccer

= Baseball

Geography

Geography *(jee-AH-gruh-fee)* tells us about places, weather, and shapes of the land. Geography tells us if places are wet or dry, hot or cold, flat or hilly. Geography lets us explore the world.

Different Lands

Most penguins like to live in icy places.

Locations

A location *(low-KAY-shun)* is where you find a place. People and animals live in all kinds of locations. Different locations affect how we live. A penguin could not live in the hot desert, and a camel would not last long in cold Antarctica!

Orangutans like jungles with lots of trees.

Pandas like to live in bamboo forests.

Lions like to live in warm grasslands.

Camels like to live in very dry areas called deserts.

Parrots like to live in wet rainforests.

39

Climate

Climate is the kind of weather a place has year after year. Virginia's climate is a mix of hot, humid summers and cool, wet winters.

Some locations on Earth are hot all the time, and some are very cold. Some places do not get any rain. Others get rain all the time.

Climate affects how we dress, what we eat, and how we live. People who live in the desert cannot make a snowman or go skiing!

A rainy climate

A hot, dry climate

Weather

Seasons

Seasons mark the parts of the year. Virginia has four different seasons. Some places only have a dry season or a rainy season. What is your favorite season?

SPRING brings showers, then flowers and warmer days.

SUMMER in the sun is so much fun. Playing outside is the best!

Leaves turn yellow, red, and orange in the FALL.

Cold and snowy WINTER days are full of frosty fun.

Spring, Summer, Fall, and Winter

The Places We Live

Surroundings

The land and water all around us are called our physical surroundings *(FIZZ-ick-ul • sir-OUN-dings).* Our surroundings affect the way we live and how we move from place to place.

Here are some different physical surroundings:

Snowy mountains

A hot desert

Flat farmlands

A tropical island

WHERE you live affects HOW you live.

	Cold places	**Hot places**
The clothes we wear	 Hats, mittens, and boots are good for snowy days.	 In the heat many people wear light clothes.
The foods we eat	 Hot soup and cocoa warm tummies on cold days.	 Ice cream and cold drinks help cool you on hot days.
The houses we live in	 People need heat and strong roofs to keep out snow.	 Homes with lots of windows can catch cool breezes.
The ways we play	 In the cold mountains you can ski and snowboard.	 In warm places you can sail and swim.

clothing   shelter   food   water

Needs are things you must have to live. You must have a home to live in. You must have clothes to protect you. You must have food and water to keep you alive.

CHAPTER 7

Things We Need and Want

Wants are things you do not really need to live. Wants are different from needs. You might want a dog. You might want to eat a banana split for dinner.

List all the things you need to live. Are any of your needs and wants the same?

Goods are the things that people make or use to satisfy our needs and wants. Goods are things we can hold and use like books, bikes, boots, and yummy donuts.

Goods and Services

Services are jobs people do for others that fill our wants and needs. People with service jobs teach us, put out fires, build things, and even save lives!

Doctor

Police

Teacher

Builder

Firefighter

Money

To get all the things we want and need, we use money. We get money by working for it. Kids do chores. Grownups do really big chores called jobs.

Buyers

With money in our hands, we are ready to buy things. We can go shopping for goods and services.

Shopping

Sellers

Sellers have all sorts of things for us to buy, from fruit to books to socks.

People are sellers when they get money for the work they do or for the goods and services they offer.

Sellers are buyers too. The owner of this fruit store will use the money she makes to buy food and clothing for her family.

People cannot have *all* the goods and services they want.
They have to choose.

People must choose some things and give up others. This boy has enough money for only one of these things. He must make a choice. Which would you choose?

Making Choices

CHAPTER 9 Spending and Saving

Spend It Now?

There are so many things to buy! We spend money to buy all sorts of goods and services such as books, ice cream, haircuts, and toys.

Save It for Later?

If you don't have enough money to buy something you really want, what can you do? Save it!

Put your money in a safe place like a bank. Add more money to it when you can. You can save money for college, a car, or even a house.

CHAPTER 10

Why We Have Rules

A **citizen** *(SIT-eh-zin)* is a member of a community.

A good citizen always follows the **rules** and helps others.

Rules keep us safe. Rules protect our rights.

Rules make sure people are treated fairly.

Here are some good rules to follow: ➡️

STOP

Be Good!

1. Play fairly.

2. Be a good sport.

3. Help others.

4. Be respectful.

5. Obey the law.

6. Have self-control.

7. Work hard.

8. Tell the truth.

9. Be responsible.

What do you think of when you hear the word "America"? Do you think of our flag—bright red, white, and blue?

Do you think of the Statue of Liberty with her big crown? Do you think of an eagle flying high in the sky?

11 We Love America!

Patriots (PAY-tree-etts) are people who love their country. Patriots are soldiers, sailors, and even boys and girls just like you. Being patriotic means that you will always respect America.

Patriotic Symbols

Symbols *(SIM-bulls)* are pictures or things that stand for something else. America has many symbols.

When we see these symbols, we always think patriotic thoughts.

The American Flag

The Statue of Liberty, in New York City

The Washington Monument in Washington, DC.

The Bald Eagle

53

Stars and Stripes

The United States flag tells a story.

Everything on it is a symbol and has a meaning.

People have risked their lives to save our flag.

Count the stripes on our flag. There are 13 in all— 7 red, and 6 white. The stripes stand for the 13 original states when our country began.

Count the stars. There are 50 white stars on a blue background. The stars are symbols of the 50 states that make up America today.

This Virginia statue honors the brave Marines who kept our flag flying in times of war.

UNCOMMON VALOR WAS A COMMON VIRTUE

The Pledge of Allegiance

We show respect for our flag with a great tradition *(tra-DISH-un)*. Many of us say the Pledge of Allegiance *(uh-LEE-jense)* every day.

What is allegiance? It is a very big word that means we will be loyal to the United States. It means that we will always respect and love our flag and our country.

I pledge allegiance to the flag of the United States of America and to the Republic for which it stands, one nation under God, indivisible, with liberty and justice for all.

All Together

People have come from all over the world to live together in Virginia. They have come from almost every continent. Some have only been here a few weeks. Others have been here for a very long time.

56

Virginia's towns and cities are filled with people who have come from faraway lands.
They bring all sorts of talents with them.

The police officer moved here from South America, the chef from Africa, the doctor from Asia, and the dancer from Europe. They all help make life in Virginia a little safer, a lot better, and more fun.

In Our Towns

Someday you will have a job. There are so many from which to pick! Do you know what you want to do when you are a grownup?

The Things We Share

A **tradition** *(tra-DISH-un)* or **custom** is something special that you and your family do every year, at a certain time, in a certain way. Many traditions from all over the world have become part of our lives.

Traditions

As people come to America, they bring all sorts of good things with them to share— yummy foods, cool music, and fun holidays. These are their customs and traditions. Pizza, piñatas, and banjos are just a few things that came to America from other places.

Holidays

Holidays are such fun! Thanksgiving is an American holiday. Each culture also has its own special holidays with great traditions— foods, games, songs, and symbols.

Kwanzaa honors African roots with many symbols.

Chanukah brings eight nights of candles and fun.

Ramadan, a Muslim holiday of prayer, ends with a feast.

Christmas brings stockings, which were first hung on fireplaces in Europe.

Celebrate!

We all come together as Americans to celebrate *(SELL-uh-brate)* July 4, our Independence Day.

Let's Review

We have learned so many things this year!

Past–things that took place long ago

Transportation– cars, planes, trains, boats

Communities–places we live, work, and go to school

George Washington– "Father of our Country"

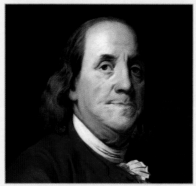

Benjamin Franklin– a great thinker

Abraham Lincoln– "Honest Abe"

George Washington Carver– a man of science

Columbus Day– an October holiday

Presidents' Day– a February holiday

Independence Day–
The 4th of July

Globe–a round model
of the Earth

Map–a flat drawing of
all or part of the Earth

Geography–places, shapes,
and weather of the world

Physical surroundings–
seas, mountains, deserts

Needs–water,
food, clothes, shelter

Wants–things you do not
need to live

Goods–things that satisfy
needs and wants

Services–jobs people do
to fill our wants and needs

Patriotic Symbols–flags,
bald eagle, Statue of Liberty

Pledge of Allegiance–a
promise to respect America

Traditions–special foods,
games, songs, and symbols

Index

America is not like a blanket–
one piece of unbroken cloth.

America is more like a quilt–
many patches, many pieces,
many colors, many sizes,
all woven together
by a common thread.

–Rev. Jesse Jackson

Resources

ADDITIONAL READING

Fox, Mem. *Whoever You Are.* Voyager Books

Kuklin, Susan. *How My Family Lives in America.* Alladin Books

Discovery Library American Symbols Series from Rourke Book Company. Titles include: *The American Flag, The American Eagle, The Statue of Liberty*.

National Holidays from Pebble Books. Titles include: *Independence Day, Martin Luther King Jr. Day,* and *Presidents' Day*.

Loewen, Nancy. *Cash, Credit Cards, or Checks.* Picture Window Books

First Biographies from Pebble Books/Capstone Press. Titles include: Rustad, Martha. *George Washington Carver.* Schaefer, Lola M. *Benjamin Franklin.*

Nelson, Robin. *From Peanut To Peanut Butter.* Lerner Publishing.

ONLINE RESOURCES

http://www.vahistorical.org
A wonderful source with lots of archival artwork to download for classroom display

http://k3hss.pwnet.org
completely correlated with the Virginia SOLS

http://www.alplm.org/timeline/timeline.html
This animated interactive timeline was created by the Lincoln Museum and Presidential Library

DON'T MISS...

Our World: Then & Now: Activities and Assessments. A sturdy binder with 48 pages of reproducibles, graphic organizers, activities and assessments is included FREE with every 25-book set of the *Our World* books.

PICTURE CREDITS

Every effort has been made to insure that this listing is complete and accurate and that appropriate credit has been given and permissions obtained. In the event of any ommisions or errors, the publisher will endeavor to correct said errors or ommisions in the next printing. All photos and illustrations listed below are copyrighted by the respective providers. Page 1: (L) National Archives, (R) Photodisc. Page 2; Rubbeball. Page 3; (TR) Photodisc, (ML) Photodisc, (BR)Corbis. Page 4; (L) Hulton Archive, (R) Corbis. Page 5; (L) Rubberball, (R) Photodisc. Page 6; All Corbis. Page 7; (T) Virginia Beach Public Schools, (B) Rubberball. Page 8; (T) Superstock, (B) Corel. Page 9; (T) City of Richmond, (B) MSA. Page 10; (T) Corbis, (B) National Archive. Page 11; (T) Corel, (B) United States Air Force. Page 12; (BL) National Archive, (BR) Corbis. Page 13; (L) Stone, (R) Taxi. Page 14; (L) Corbis, (M) National Portrait Gallery, (R) Lincoln Museum, Springfield, IL. Page 15, (L) Corel, (M) Photodisc, (R) Rubberball. CHAPTER 2, Page 16; National Archive. Page 17; (T) National Archive, (M) Metropolitan Museum of Art. Page 18; All Corbis. Page 19, (M) Cigna, (B) American Philosophical Society. Page 20; (L) United States Navel Acadamy. (R) National Archives. Page 21, (T) National Archives, (M) Lincoln Museum and Library, (B) National Archives. Page 22; (L) Gettyone, (R) Painting by Michele Anderson. Page 23; (T) Corbis, (M) Photodisc, (B) MSA. CHAPTER 4, Page 24; Corbis. Page 25; (TL) Metropolitan Museum of Art, New York, (TR) United States Navel Acadamy, (M) Photodisc. Page 27; (TR) Photodisc, (M) Photodisc, (B) Corbis. CHAPTER 5, Page 28; (TR) Digital Vision, (B) Stone. Page 29; (T) MSA (TM) Rubberball, (B) The Image Bank. Page 30; MSA. page 31; Gobes: Digital Vision, (T) Rubberball, (B) Brand X. Page 32; Stockbyte. Page 33; MSA. Page 35; (T) MSA, (BL) Photodisc, (BM) Corel, (BR) Photodisc. Page 36; (TL) Brand X. CHAPTER 6, Page 38, (L) Digital Vision, (R) Corel. page 39; (T) Corbis RF, (ML) Corel, (MR) Corbis RF, (BL) Corbis, (BR) Corel. Page 40; (BL) The Image Bank, (MB) Corbis RF, (BR) The Image Bank. Page 41; (TL) Photodisc, (TR) Brand X, (BL) Photodisc, (BR) Corel. Page 42; (ML) Corel, (BL) Photodisc MR) Photodisc (BR) Corel. Page 43, Clockwise from TL, Digital Vision, Corbis, Corel, Photodisc, Corel, Corel, Corbis, Comstock. CHAPTER 7, Page 44; (T from L to R) Photodisc, Brand X, Corel, Photodisc. (MR) Photodisc, (ML) Photodisc, (BR) Photodisc. Page 45, (T from L to R) Corel, Brand X, Photodisc, Digital Vision, Photodisc, (B) All photos Rubberball. Page 46; (TL) MSA, (BL) Photodisc, (TR) Photodisc. Page 47, (T) Stone, (BR) Corbis. CHAPTER 8, Page 48; (B) The Image Bank. (BL) Corbis. CHAPTER 9, Page 49, All Photodisc. CHAPTER 10, Page 50; All Rubberball. Page 51; (Clockwise from TL) Comstock, Brand X, Brand X, Corbis, Photodisc, Corbis, Photodisc, Corel, Corbis. CHAPTER 11, Page 52; (TL) Corbis, (BR) Stone. Page 53; (TR) Photodisc, (MR) Corel, (BR) Corel, (BL) Digital Vision. Page 54; (TR) Photodisc, (BR) Digitial Vision. Page 55, Rubberball. CHAPTER 12, Page 56; (TL) Stone, (TR) Corel, (BR) Corel, (BL) Corbis. Page 57, Corbis. Page 58; All Photodisc. Page 59; TR, Corbis, (ML) Photodisc, (MCL) Photodisc, (MCR) Naqshbandi-Haqqani Sufi Mosque, (MR) Photodisc. Page 60; (Clockwise from TL) MSA, National Archives, City of Richmond, United States Naval Academy, Photodisc, Corbis, National Archives-Michele Anderson, National Portrait Gallery, Cochran Gallery. Page 61; (From TL clockwise) Corbis, Photodisc, MSA, Corel, Corbis, Corbis, Digital Vision, Corel, Photodisc, Corel, Corel, Corbis. Page 63, (From Top to Bottom, L to R), Rubberball, Rubberball, Corel, Corel, Rubberball, Photodisc, Photodisc, Photodisc, Rubberball, Corel, Corel, Photodisc, Corel, Corel, Corel, Photodisc, Rubberball, Corel, Corel, Photodisc, Rubberball, Corel, Photodisc, Rubberball, Corel, Corel, Photodisc, Rubberball, Photodisc, Corel, Corel, Photodisc, Photodisc, Corel, Rubberball, Rubberball, Corel, Corel, Corel, Corel, Rubberball, Photodisc, Photodisc, Corel, Rubberball, Photodisc, Corel, Corel, Corel, Photodisc, Photodisc, Corel. FRONT COVER; (BL) Hulton Archive, (TR) Antique map from a private collection, (BR) Digital Vision. BACK COVER; (BL) United States Naval Academy, (BM) Corbis, (BR) Digital Vision.